About
Skill Builders
Handwriting

by Clareen Arnold

Welcome to RBP Books' Skill Builders series. The Skill Builders series is designed to make learning fun and rewarding.

The Skill Builders Contemporary Cursive handwriting exercises were developed to provide parents and teachers with a tool for reinforcing handwriting skills as children progress from printing into cursive. Parents should plan on helping their children with these pages.

This book begins with instruction pages for making each of the letters in the Contemporary Cursive style. These include a tracing exercise to give students the chance to shape each letter in its uppercase and lowercase form, followed by space they can use to practice writing the letter on their own. From there, the book moves on to word and sentence formation. There is a practice page for each letter with words that begin with that letter, followed by a practice page for each letter with words that begin with that letter in a sentence.

Learning is more effective when approached with an element of fun and enthusiasm. That's why the Skill Builders combine academically sound exercises with engaging graphics and entertaining themes—to make reviewing basic skills fun and effective, for both you and your budding scholars.

W9-AAP-829

Table of Contents

m m m

M M M

m m m

M M M

n n n

N N N

n n n

N N N

$\mathcal{A}$ $\mathcal{A}$ — — — —

a a — — — —

$\mathcal{A}nn$ $\mathcal{A}nn$

ant ant

an an

am am

are are

ate ate

air air

Al the alligator
ate an apple.
Al the alligator
ate an apple.

17

$\mathcal{B}$ $\mathcal{B}$ — —

b b — —

Bob Bob

bus bus

big big

bat bat

bed bed

bird bird

bear bear

Bear bounces
the beach ball.

Bear bounces
the beach ball.

C C _____ _____

c c _____ _____

Carl Carl

car car

cat cat

cow cow

can can

cup cup

calf calf

Cow watches
the crab crawl.

Cow watches
the crab crawl.

21

D D _____ _____ _____

d d _____ _____ _____

Don Don

day day

did did

do do

dry dry

dog dog

duck duck

Dolphin dives
for doughnuts.

Dolphin dives
for doughnuts.

$\mathcal{E}$ $\mathcal{E}$ - - - - - - - - - -

e e - - - - - - - - - -

Eva Eva

eat eat

each each

eye eye

ear ear

elf elf

eel eel

Ed Elephant sits

on an egg.

Ed Elephant sits

on an egg.

F F

f f

Fred Fred

fan fan

frog frog

fur fur

fig fig

fox fox

fish fish

Find five fat,
freckled fish.

Find five fat,
freckled fish.

$\mathcal{G}$ $\mathcal{G}$

g g

Greg   Greg

gas   gas

gym   gym

get   get

go   go

gum   gum

give   give

Giraffe slips on
giant gumballs.
Giraffe slips on
giant gumballs.

$\mathcal{H}$ $\mathcal{H}$ $\mathcal{H}$

h h

$\mathcal{H}al$ $\mathcal{H}al$

hen hen

ham ham

hog hog

hit hit

hay hay

hat hat

Is Horse hiding
in the hay?
Is Horse hiding
in the hay?

$\mathcal{I}$ $\mathcal{I}$

i i

$\mathcal{I}ke$ $\mathcal{I}ke$

it it

if if

in in

$itch$ $itch$

ivy ivy

ice ice

Ike Iguana eats
icky insects.

Ike Iguana eats
icky insects.

$\mathcal{J}$ $\mathcal{J}$ — — —

j j — — —

Jay Jay

jar jar

job job

jam jam

jail jail

jug jug

jet jet

Jaguar juggles with Jellyfish.

$\mathcal{K}$ $\mathcal{K}$ — — —

k k — — —

$\mathcal{K}ay$ $\mathcal{K}ay$

kid kid

$keep$ $keep$

key key

$knit$ $knit$

keg keg

$kite$ $kite$

Katie Kangaroo
flies a kite.
Katie Kangaroo
flies a kite.

$\mathcal{L}$ $\mathcal{L}$ $\mathcal{L}$

l l l

Lou Lou

leg leg

let let

lid lid

log log

lips lips

lion lion

Llama laughs
at Lizard's joke.
Llama laughs
at Lizard's joke.

M M

m m

Meg Meg

mad mad

men men

mug mug

mix mix

mop mop

mill mill

Mike Mouse
dances to music.
Mike Mouse
dances to music.

$\mathcal{N}$ $\mathcal{N}$

n n

Nate Nate

nut nut

nap nap

not not

nine nine

net net

nest nest

No nest needs
ninety nuts.
No nest needs
ninety nuts.

$\mathcal{O}$ $\mathcal{O}$ $\mathcal{O}$

o o

Otis Otis

old old

out out

one one

ox ox

oil oil

owl owl

Ostrich likes to watch Octopus.

P P P _ _ _ _

p p p _ _ _ _

Peg Peg _ _ _

put put _ _ _

pan pan _ _ _

pen pen _ _ _

pop pop _ _ _

play play _ _ _

pig pig

Pink Pig hides

in a pumpkin.

Pink Pig hides

in a pumpkin.

$\mathcal{Q}$ $\mathcal{Q}$ —— —— ——

q q —— ——

$\mathcal{Q}uinn$ $\mathcal{Q}uinn$

quail quail

quick quick

quiet quiet

quit quit

quest quest

queen queen

Quiet Quail

quilts quickly.

Quiet Quail

quilts quickly.

$\mathcal{R}$ $\mathcal{R}$

r r

Russ Russ

red red

ran ran

rug rug

rock rock

ride ride

rabbit rabbit

Rooster and Rat

romp in the rain.

Rooster and Rat

romp in the rain.

Contemporary Cursive—RBP3071

S S

s s

Sam   Sam

sad   sad

sky   sky

she   she

sun   sun

sit   sit

seal   seal

Snake tells

Skunk a secret.

Snake tells

Skunk a secret.

$\mathcal{T}$ $\mathcal{T}$ $\mathcal{T}$

t t t

Ted Ted

tag tag

tell tell

ten ten

two two

tub tub

turtle turtle

Tom Tiger took
a trip to Texas.
Tom Tiger took
a trip to Texas.

U *U* — — — — —

u *u* — — — — —

Uma Uma

use use

up up

ugly ugly

ultra ultra

under under

unicorn unicorn

Unicorn is under the umbrella.

Unicorn is under the umbrella.

$\mathcal{V}$ $\mathcal{V}$

v v

Vera Vera

very very

voice voice

van van

view view

vase vase

vacuum vacuum

Vulture received

a valentine.

Vulture received

a valentine.

Will _____ _____

w w _____ _____

Wes Wes _____

will will _____

wag wag

web web

wasp wasp

wax wax

wolf wolf

Whale was in
a whirlwind.
Whale was in
a whirlwind.

X X X

x x x

Xavier Xavier

X-ray X-ray

xylophone

xylophone

Xerox Xerox

Rex Fox looks

at a xylophone.

Rex Fox looks

at a xylophone.

63

$\mathcal{Y}$ $\mathcal{Y}$

y y

Yeda Yeda

yell yell

yes yes

you you

yet yet

yeah yeah

yarn yarn

Yak plays with
yellow yarn.
Yak plays with
yellow yarn.

$\mathcal{Z}$ $\mathcal{Z}$ $\mathcal{Z}$

$\mathcal{Z}$ $\mathcal{Z}$

Zeke Zeke

zap zap

zig zig

zag zag

zoom zoom

zebra zebra

zipper zipper

Zookeepers feed
Zebra at the zoo.

Zookeepers feed
Zebra at the zoo.

1

One   One   One

2

Two   Two   Two

3

Three   Three

68

4

Four   Four

5   5   5

Five   Five

6   6   6

Six   Six   Six

Contemporary Cursive—RBP3071

7 7 7 7 — — — 7

Seven   Seven

8 8 8 8 — — — —

Eight   Eight

9 9 9 9 — — — 9

Nine   Nine

10   10

Ten   Ten   Ten

11   11

Eleven   Eleven

12   12

Twelve   Twelve

Colors

red

yellow

blue

green

black

brown

orange

purple

Shapes

line

oval

star

circle

square

triangle

diamond

rectangle

Food

pizza

soup

beans

milk

eggs

apple

toast

burrito

corn

juice

yogurt

bread

cereal

meat

cheese

nuts

peas

January

February

March

April

May

June

July

August

September

October

November

December

Monday

Tuesday

Wednesday

Thursday

Friday

Saturday

Sunday

week

month

year

birthday

night

day

minute

hour

noon

morning

afternoon

evening